About Skill Builders Handwriting

by Clareen Arnold

Welcome to RBP Books' Skill Builders series. Like our Summer Bridge Activities collection, the Skill Builders series is designed to make learning both fun and rewarding.

The Skill Builders Modern Manuscript handwriting exercises were developed to provide parents and teachers with a tool for reinforcing handwriting skills and facilitating progression from printing into cursive. A child who has mastered printing in this script, using correct size and spacing, can easily change to cursive writing by connecting the lead-in line from one letter to the next. Parents should plan on helping their children with these pages.

This book begins with instruction pages for making each of the letters in the Modern Manuscript style. These include a tracing exercise to give students the chance to shape each letter in its uppercase and lowercase form, followed by space they can use to practice writing the letter on their own. From there, the book moves on to word and sentence formation. There is a practice page for each letter with words that begin with that letter, followed by a practice page for each letter with words that begin with that letter in a sentence.

Learning is more effective when approached with an element of fun and enthusiasm—just as most children approach life. That's why the Skill Builders combine entertaining and academically sound exercises with eye-catching graphics and fun themes—to make reviewing basic skills fun and effective, for both you and your budding scholars.

Table of Contents

ABC DN Manuscript font family used by permission of Fonts4Teachers.

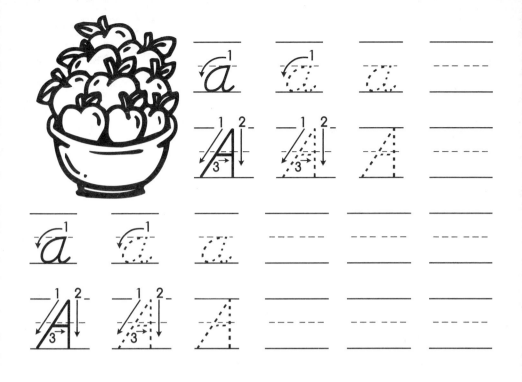

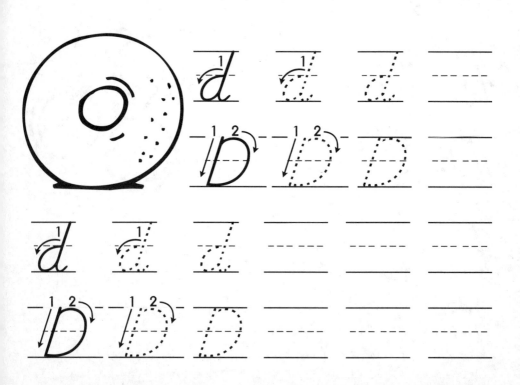

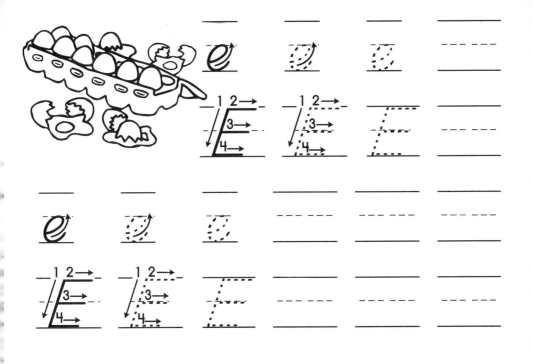

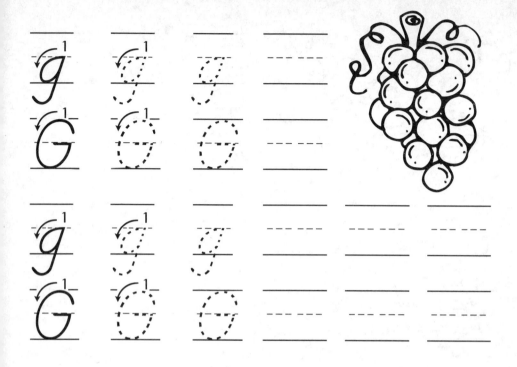

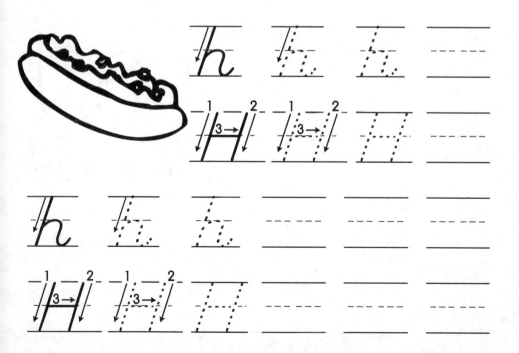

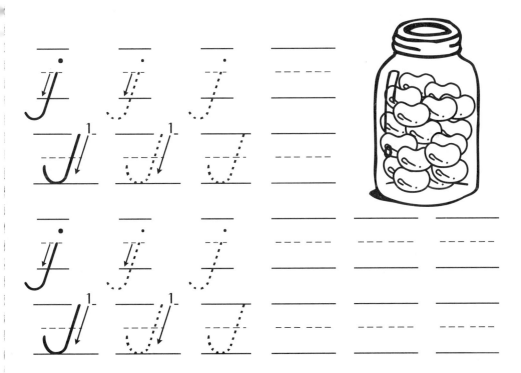

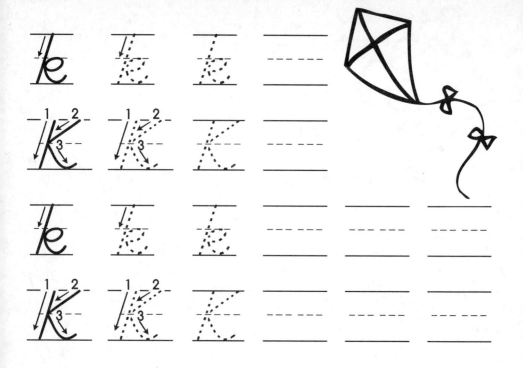

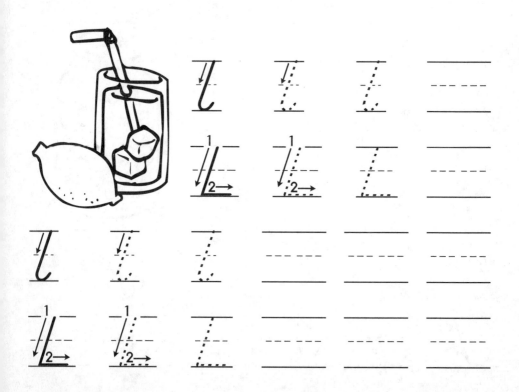

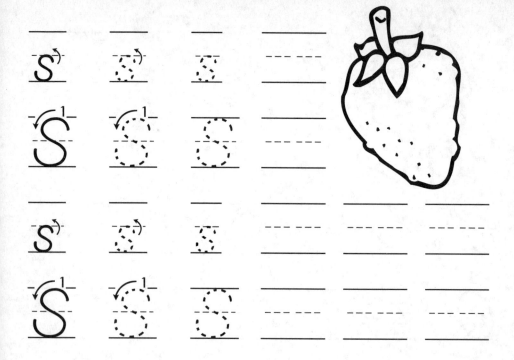

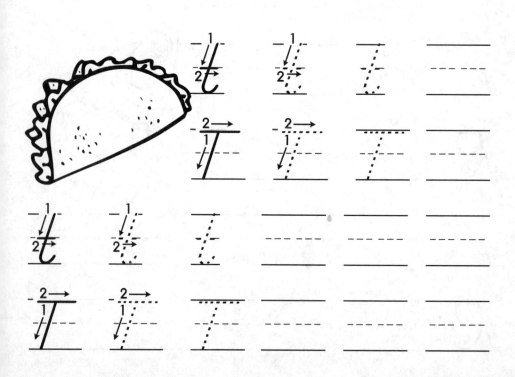

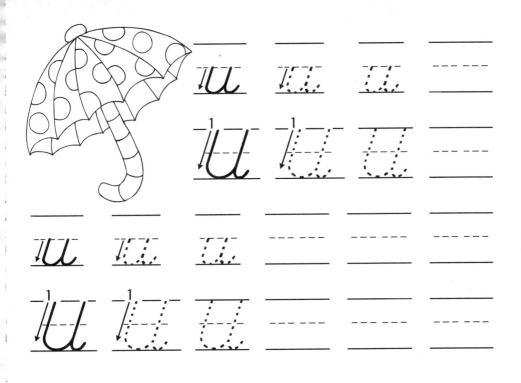

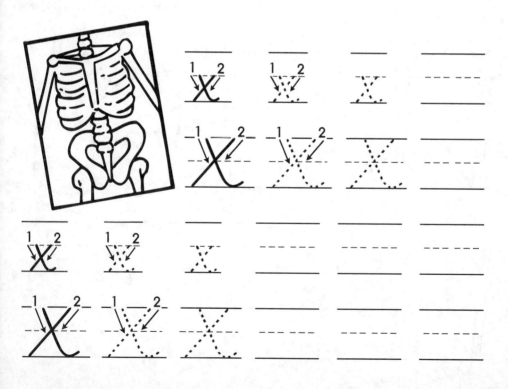

    ©RBP Books

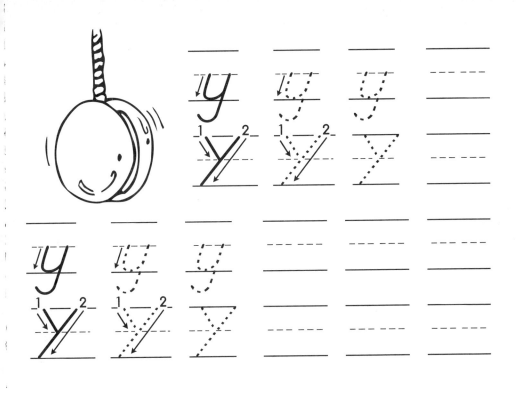

A

a

Ann Ann

ant ant

an an

am am

are are

ate ate

air air

Al the alligator
ate an apple.
Al the alligator
ate an apple.

B B B _ _ _ _
b b _ _ _ _

Bob *Bob*

bus *bus*

big *big*

bat *bat*

bed *bed*

bird *bird*

bear *bear*

Bear bounces
the beach ball.

Bear bounces
the beach ball.

C C _ _

c c _ _

Carl Carl

car car

cat cat

cow cow

can can

cup cup

calf calf

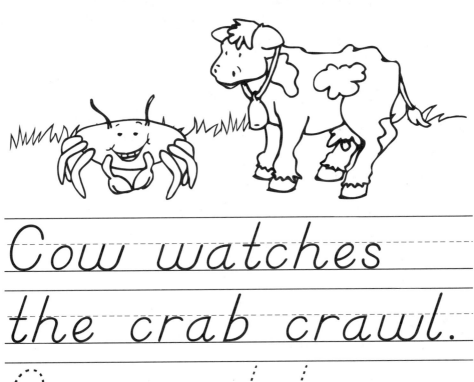

Cow watches
the crab crawl.

Cow watches
the crab crawl.

D D
d d

Don Don

day day

did did

do do

dry dry

dog dog

duck duck

Dolphin dives

for doughnuts.

Dolphin dives

for doughnuts.

E E - - -

e e - - -

Eva Eva

eat eat

each each

eye eye

ear ear

elf elf

eel eel

Ed Elephant

sits on an egg.

Ed Elephant

sits on an egg.

F F F F F

f f f f f

Fred Fred

fan fan

frog frog

fur fur

fig fig

fox fox

fish fish

Find five fat,
freckled fish.

Find five fat,
freckled fish.

G G

g g

Greg Greg

gas gas

gym gym

get get

go go

gum gum

give give

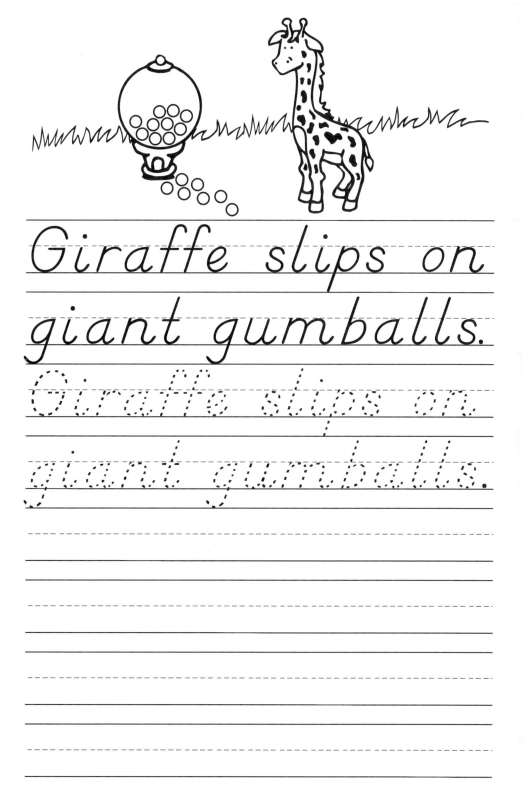

Giraffe slips on
giant gumballs.

Giraffe slips on
giant gumballs.

H H - - - -

h h - - - -

Hal Hal

hen hen

ham ham

hog hog

hit hit

hay hay

hat hat

Is Horse hiding
in the hay?

Is Horse hiding
in the hay?

I I --- --- ---

i i --- --- ---

Ike Ike

it it

if if

in in

itch itch

ivy ivy

ice ice

Ike Iguana eats icky insects.

Ike Iguana eats icky insects.

J J J

j j j

Jay Jay

jar jar

job job

jam jam

jail jail

jug jug

jet jet

Jaguar juggles
with Jellyfish.

Jaguar juggles
with Jellyfish.

K K
k k

Kay Kay
kid kid
keep keep
key key
knit knit
keg keg
kite kite

Katie Kangaroo
flies a kite.

Katie Kangaroo
flies a kite.

L L L L L

l l l l l

Lou Lou

leg leg

let let

lid lid

log log

lips lips

lion lion

Llama laughs
at Lizard's joke.

Llama laughs
at Lizard's joke.

M M M _ _ _ _ _ _

m m m _ _ _ _ _

Meg Meg

mad mad

men men

mug mug

mix mix

mop mop

mill mill

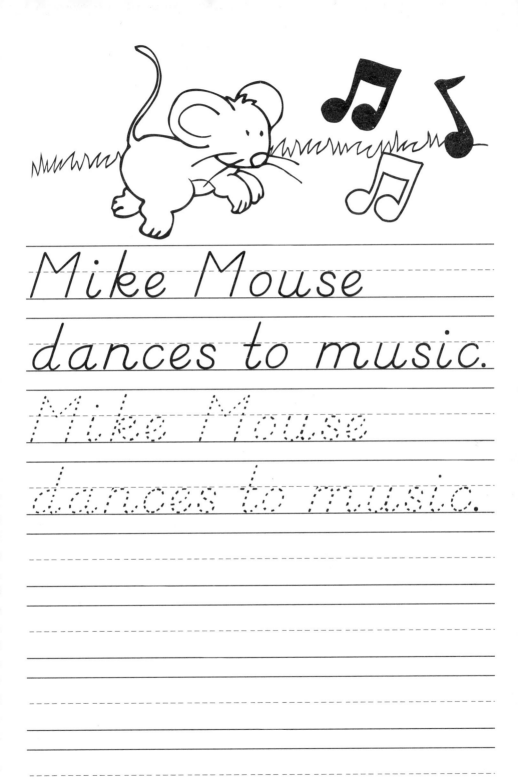

Mike Mouse

dances to music.

Mike Mouse

dances to music.

N N N

n n

Nate Nate

nut nut

nap nap

not not

nine nine

net net

nest nest

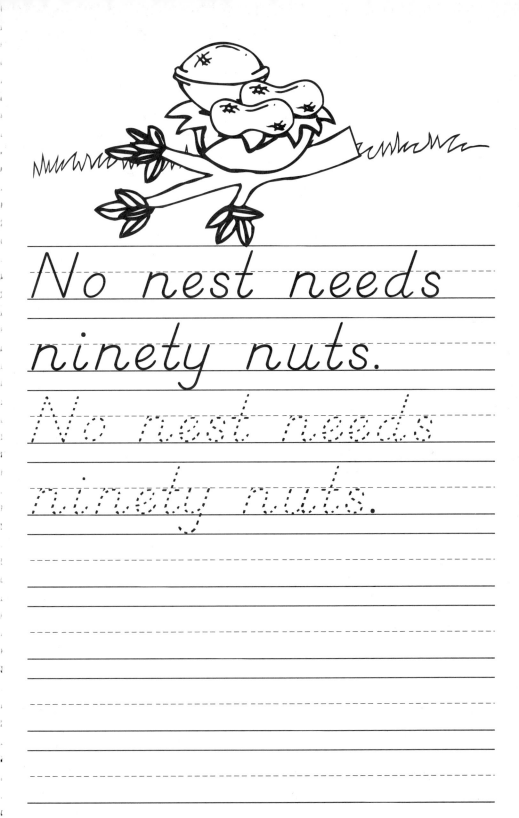

No nest needs
ninety nuts.

No nest needs
ninety nuts.

O O _____ _____

o o _____ _____

Otis Otis

old old

out out

one one

ox ox

oil oil

owl owl

Ostrich likes to
watch Octopus.

Ostrich likes to
watch Octopus.

P P P - - - - -

p p p - - - - -

Peg Peg

put put

pan pan

pen pen

pop pop

play play

pig pig

Pink Pig hides

in a pumpkin.

Pink Pig hides

in a pumpkin.

Q Q - - - - - - - - - -

q q - - - - - - - - - -

Quinn   *Quinn*

quail   *quail*

quick   *quick*

quiet   *quiet*

quit   *quit*

quest   *quest*

queen   *queen*

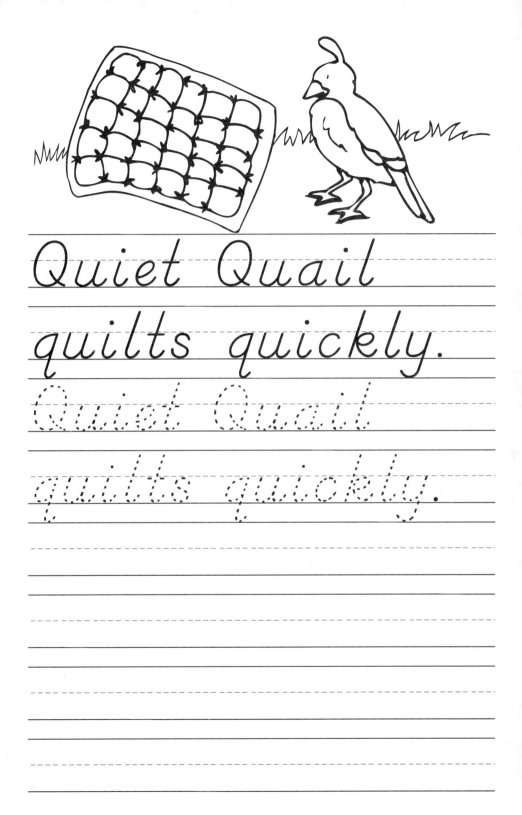

Quiet Quail

quilts quickly.

Quiet Quail

quilts quickly.

R R - - - -

r r - - - -

Russ Russ

red red

ran ran

rug rug

rock rock

ride ride

rabbit rabbit

Rooster and Rat

romp in the rain.

Rooster and Rat

romp in the rain.

S S _____ _____
s s _____ _____

Sam Sam

sad sad

sky sky

she she

sun sun

sit sit

seal seal

Snake tells

Skunk a secret.

Snake tells

Skunk a secret.

T T — — — —

t t — — — —

Ted Ted

tag tag

tell tell

ten ten

two two

tub tub

turtle turtle

Tom Tiger took
a trip to Texas.
Tom Tiger took
a trip to Texas.

U u ⌐ ⌐ ⌐

u u ⌐ ⌐ ⌐

Uma *Uma*

use *use*

up *up*

ugly *ugly*

ultra *ultra*

under *under*

unicorn *unicorn*

Unicorn is under
the umbrella.
Unicorn is under
the umbrella.

V V – – –

V V – – –

Vera Vera

very very

voice voice

van van

view view

vase vase

vacuum vacuum

Vulture received
a valentine.

Vulture received
a valentine.

W W W W

w w w

Wes Wes

will will

wag wag

web web

wasp wasp

wax wax

wolf wolf

Whale was in
a whirlwind.

Whale was in
a whirlwind.

X X

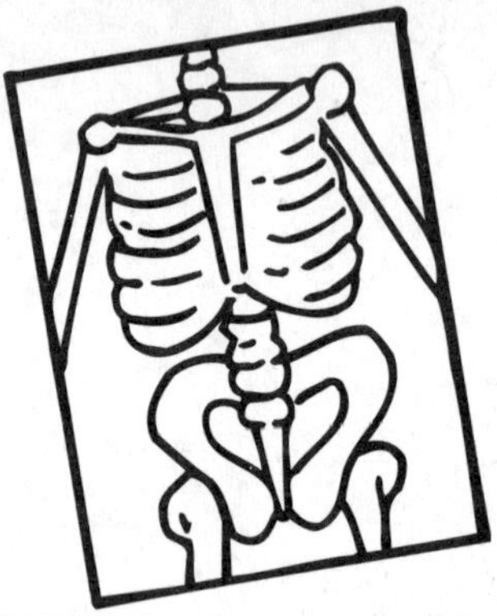

X X

Xavier _Xavier_

X-ray _X-ray_

xylophone

xylophone

Xerox _Xerox_

Rex Fox looks
at a xylophone.
Rex Fox looks
at a xylophone.

Modern Manuscript—RBP0261

Y Y Y - - - - - - - -

y y - - - - - - - - -

Yeda Yeda

yell yell

yes yes

you you

yet yet

yeah yeah

yarn yarn

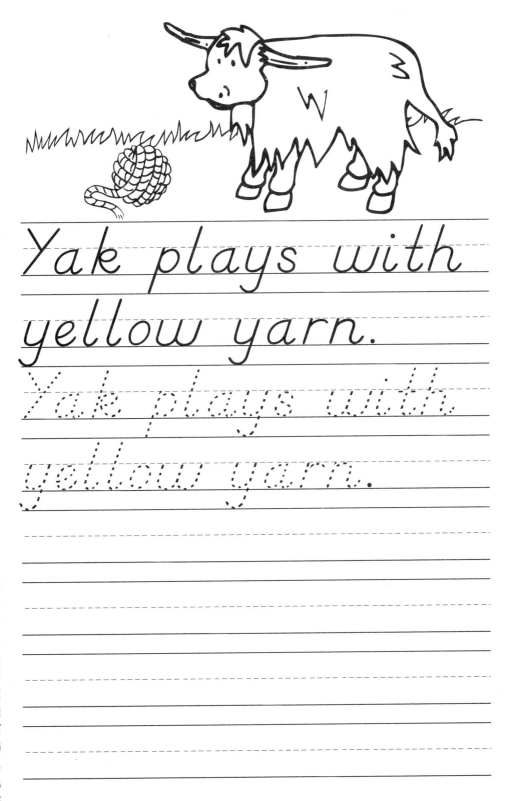

Yak plays with
yellow yarn.

Yak plays with
yellow yarn.

Z

^{1}→ Z z ‾ ‾ ‾ ‾ ‾ ‾

→ Z z

Zeke Zeke

zap zap

zig zig

zag zag

zoom zoom

zebra zebra

zipper zipper

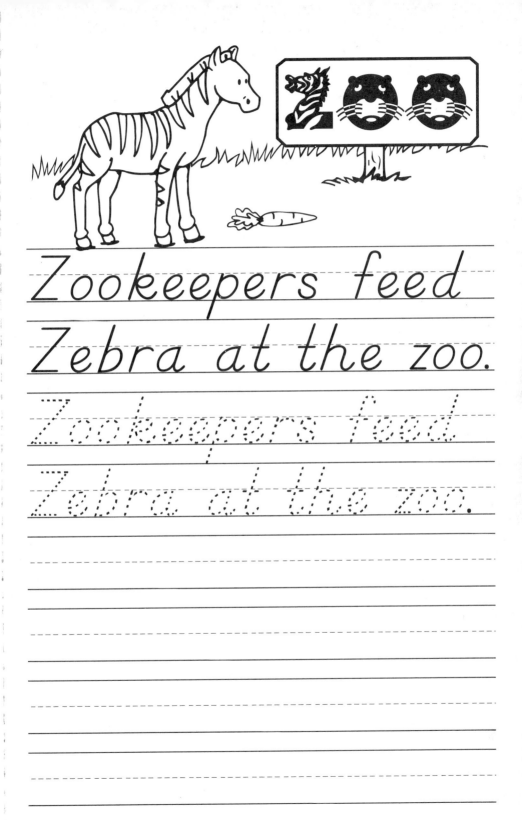

Zookeepers feed
Zebra at the zoo.

Zookeepers feed
Zebra at the zoo.

1

One   One   One

2

Two   Two   Two

3

Three   Three

7 7 7

Seven Seven

8 8 8

Eight Eight

9 9 9

Nine Nine

Finish

10   10

Ten   Ten   Ten

11   11

Eleven   Eleven

12   12   12

Twelve   Twelve

Colors

red

yellow

blue

green

black

brown

orange

purple

Shapes

line

oval

star

circle

square

triangle

diamond

rectangle

Modern Manuscript—RBP0261

Food

pizza

soup

beans

milk

eggs

apple

toast

burrito

corn

juice

yogurt

bread

cereal

meat

cheese

nuts

peas

January

February

March

April

May

June

July

August

September

October

November

December

Monday

Tuesday

Wednesday

Thursday

Friday

Saturday

Sunday

week

month

year

birthday

night

day

minute

hour

noon

morning

afternoon

evening